No Town Called We

Also by Nikki Reimer

[sic]

*DOWNVERSE**

*My Heart Is a Rose Manhattan**

* Published by Talonbooks

NO
TOWN
CALLED WE

POEMS

NIKKI REIMER

TALONBOOKS

Talonbooks
9259 Shaughnessy Street, Vancouver, British Columbia, Canada v6p 6r4
talonbooks.com

Talonbooks is located on xʷməθkʷəy̓əm, Sḵwx̱wú7mesh, and səlilwətaɫ Lands.

First printing: 2023

Typeset in Arno
Printed and bound in Canada on 100% post-consumer recycled paper

Interior and cover by Typesmith
Cover artwork by Nikki Reimer

Talonbooks acknowledges the financial support of the Canada Council for the Arts, the Government of Canada through the Canada Book Fund, and the Province of British Columbia through the British Columbia Arts Council and the Book Publishing Tax Credit.

LIBRARY AND ARCHIVES CANADA CATALOGUING IN PUBLICATION

Title: No town called we : poems / Nikki Reimer.
Names: Reimer, Nikki, author.
Identifiers: Canadiana 20230455654 | ISBN 9781772015492 (softcover)
Classification: LCC PS8635.E463 N6 2023 | DDC C811/.6—dc23

For Amy and Chandler, home poets We

The *outside* is not another space that resides beyond a determinate space, but rather, it is the passage, the exteriority that gives it access – in a word, it is its face, its *eidos*.

The threshold is not, in this sense, another thing with respect to the limit; it is, so to speak, the experience of the limit itself, the experience of being-*within* an *outside*. This ek-stasis is the gift that singularity gathers from the empty hands of humanity.

—GIORGIO AGAMBEN

The Coming Community, translated by Michael Hardt (1993)

While sensation is not transferable, and hence not social, desires and beliefs are intrinsically social, that is transferable, communicable, circulatory.

—TIZIANA TERRANOVA

After the Internet: Digital Networks between Capital and the Common (2022)

No Town Called Poetry

The Daily We

One Poet Always Lies

The iLL Symbolic

No Town Called Poetry

We Wonder If i Will Ever Manage to Write a Poem about Heat Death

Sparring kangaroos were dancing
rain-joy, we said.
That's fighting, said the scientist
old photo.
Koalas in renal failure
foregoing their fear
to lap water from the road were deemed
"cute." No, no, said the scientist, not "cute."
Those creatures are dying.
We'd moved on. Wombats shepherd
other critters into their burrows! Stewards of the underbrush!
Not quite right, said the scientist, wombat burrows are enormous.
Most likely the wombat was hiding in another chamber.
We'd already created a hashtag:
#WombatEmpathy will save us!

i asked the cat what comes next,
        and he said
        either the complete transformation
        of existing relationships
        or the heat death of the
        planet. One of those.

My heart's for home, relationships, kangaroos, scientists.
No time for settler logic.
No atheists in burrows, friend.
No one coming to save us.

This Is Not My Beautiful Horse

we fails good citizenship / grows wan at promos for online readings /
we cannot i will not we prefer not to / cocoon bed or marooned /
embodied ghostships / "it's not the optimal time to die" / we've
thrown out ratty towels and bedsheets / sifted detritus / vacuum robot
hums our homing beacon / we hum myself / we're underwater / the
gentle horse pressed her nose into my armpit, breathed softly onto we
face / we can't donate or sell or throw anything away / no poetry of
stasis / spouse gets up to smoke / ol' quarantinin' bean / we'd never
met that horse but she caressed we like a lover / this is not symbolic i'm
talking about a physical horse / their dad's off running with the
physical fox / back door blown open / yellow flannel sheets / we sit in
this house till it's safe to deconstruct home / what if it's never safe to
deconstruct home / as for we and my physical house / ran out of
energy to produce / beautiful content for the timeline / no town called
resilience / is that a stress hive or / not my beautiful house / too late
too soon / all keening in the death house / all quiet in the death home /
all thrumming in the death horse /

We ♥ Alberta's Ol' Symbolic

take the elevator to our second floor
apartment bust out the biodiesel
firmware use medical-grade plastic
bottles for saline nasal
rinse gotta keep those
mucus membranes clean for we
and the dust bowl, babe
run that old car all up and down
this city's sprawl we try to keep warm
through frigid prairie winters feel appropriate
guilt at the plastic produce bags we bring home
from the grocery store / forget the mesh ones
every time / we've gone full enemy-of-the-state assault vehicle
applied to be the next poet-in-residence for carbon capture
(mass species death, but make it fashion)

everything we see is: development
gently falling leaves in the inner city: development
Enoch Sales heritage home fire: development
empty condo tower on empty condo tower:
the firing of five thousand Albertan nurses in the year
2019 / nine dead from fires in New South Wales since Monday
now seventeen
now twenty-four, meanwhile:

we're busting at the seams over here:
Montana, Drake, East Village, Tuscany
new history razed for imported ideas
another thunder swing
from settler colonialism's long neoliberal tail
clearing a path for the rule of the patch:
by the patch for the patch
for the capitalist overlord bosses of our demise
for the dinosaurs who never left us

Oil and Gas Don't Love We Back

We expand
to the outskirts
and hop on the brain

fill 311,000 square feet of empty office add eleven
new communities to this windswept
granite countertop

lease the premier
wave at the layoff or give the people a
ring around this city
pockmarked full of road rage
husha husha we all fall

downed fences make bad-neigh-bours

let's build an eight-lane freeway in the middle of the freeway
let's annex every neighbouring waydowntown

all hell for a basement sure but
never stopped to ask what was underneath
did you, poet?

did you abandon your home, your family, your health or
contemplate new urban growth
wrested from the stewards of the land we never

speak of the status quo as violence
do we, poet?

when we said trains, we didn't mean
four suburban homes to every family

we blew up that inner-city hospital
and we'll fuck around and

tear down the pools empty the fire halls divert
blood from the heart to save the

extremities dirty dirty
sprawl all the way to Red Deer

no town called suburban emergency
no town called clinical sacrifice

Do You Remember When It Was 2007
and Nothing Hurt / Everyone We Loved Yet Alive?

It's quarantine day whatever
we've descended into lawless anarchy
plates have been broken, some say
we deserved it

We wanna watch the video of the golden retriever
ripping his friend's newspaper
to shreds over and over
like, bro, same

Our neighbours ring the seven o'clock
health care worker–appreciation cowbell
we wonder how many voted in
the tinpot ideologues

Let's bang pots for nurses, sure, but
show me the way to the machine
that kills fascists

Goodnight Capital

bed down for winter in the dawn of the New Detroit. been years
since we had a good hospital fire sale. i yawn ferocity on the plane.
are the rents high, someone asks. we don't know that man but i call
his cat Baby. i drink tea up and down the cafés of Plateau-Mont-
Royal. where i'm from, we'd call that mountain a bluff. don't call me.
in Baltimore a man said hey i like your style, i like your hair, Baby. in
Montréal we become Madame. in-flight wi-fi the best excuse to be
our worst selves. no town called forbearance. what year did anxiety
stop being sexy. do you like my style, Baby? do you like our hair?
that winter lymph glands swell to threaten mutiny. who's dying to
get fired. donate our pensions to oil, job funding to gas. it's winter,
again. we're in morning, again. just tuck me into this nest of pillows
and leave we here; we'll either thaw out in the winter or.

Who Do We Serve

we're a post-prairie post-winter weather eruption, another shit
blanket of snow. inside we run hot and cold. we sweat, i freeze. it's
not that we're stress eating, bloated, swollen, and constipated. where
is the music in pandemics, poet? everyone on Twitter is cough-
worried; the constant cleansing has desiccated our hands. "it's a dry
cold," the scientist said. air pressure 101.8 kPa and falling. i tune in to
the 4:30 p.m. dispatch to find out who's died. you dream about
meeting each other in airports. emails from management urge
self-care and sanity. meanwhile all our friends are out of work, and
rent is due.

No Town Called Solidarity

We push forward, we pull through
we carve out enough time
to write the words:

Here in the libertarian post-century
nothing matters if it's not scalable

At breakfast with coffee i watched
steady ice-drip from the eavestroughs
gig-work delivery drivers stop and go
four teens try and fail to jumpstart their car

On the balcony the cat takes notes for his next manifesto

Let me be the first to post
THANKS, WE HATE IT on our tombstones
being good at my job is
a sick game we
play with my self

No Town Called Poetry

No town called Human Potentiality
No town called We the Dust
No town called We Don't Work
No town called Diffuse to Nothing
No town called Landback Now
No town called Ol' Symbolic
No town called Petty Bourgeoisie
No town called Poetics of the Undercommons
No town called Hometown
No town called Antiwork
No town called No Town
No more town called Our Town
No town called Good Death
No town called Collective Safety Measures
No town called Post-Capital
No town called Era of the Spectacle
No town called the Indeterminate We
No town called Poetics of the Algorithm
No town called Whatever
No town called Whatever Whatever
No town called Illusions of the Future
No town called the Daily Me
No town called Public Transportation Investment
No town called Thin Blue Zone
No town called No-Go Lines
No town called Urban Sprawl
No town called Confluence
No town called Bulk Unsalted Peanuts
No town called Keening Doves
No town called Post-Post Death
No town of the Coming Community

No Town Called Migraine Glaze

We begin with a single-celled aura
select cravings to make us into entrepreneurs
rather than cats

Towards scotoma we come
knit one purl one looped over the cuckoo's
nested-tuna glory
Hello, Baba Yaga? i miss we
is that you, salted anxiety?
still allergic to the antiviral fish slurry?
still working the word "superannuated" into a poem?

Squint perfectly into the plastic fishbowl vision:
no medals earn prismatic sightlines
no town called crystal weather toxin

We begin one million throbbing steps to the coliseum
no wait, the vancouver Public library

Yeah, that's right
Baba Yaga belly

Thus ends every poem:
three days before her head
with her death
the cat

"We are bipedal fuckups whose cells start to eat themselves if we live too long"

Divine creation ripe gluteus maximus
more like quarantine mangosteen
indigent trauma-sludge brain
allergy-swell mouth feel but make it toxins

Everyone says yay on the internet
everyone says congratulations says eat your heart out
says quarantini says hold my beer
says hold my tear

There's no ode to the catheter, no rock anthem of the LPN,
no Netflix special devoted to the supply-chain drama
of the subpar-quality paper mask

There's no mortal return policy fifth stage of cancer

June 2022

pollen covers everything

like a climate-change murder scene

yellow handprint on the hand-me-down Dodge

the cat

dragging his leash around the yard

is no metaphor for self-imposed limitations

i'm trying to get at a definition
of responsibility:

i am trying to evict the cop
in my head

i'm trying to arrest the landlord
in my brain

So What

dear scientists, *i'm* still sorry for the narrative bent of *my* recent
writings / don't know how to make these layers of trauma into art: i
HATE NARRATIVE. the manthropocene howls. the fucking moon
is full and yesterday the cat sunk one of his claws full deep to the
bone of the scientist's pointer finger. so what? the wound formed a
white moon ringed in purple. here is the home of our poetics of the
plaintive. so what. it's a pollen-bitten pandemic dawn tinged with
the deep regret of spring. so what. *jesus* wept. the other cat pissed all
over our shoes twice today. so what. we collected the father-in-law's
things from the hospital: two pillows, pyjamas, his shaving kit. his
duffel bag a burden against my hip, my right shoulder seizing from
the weight on the sweaty walk home. what is a man's final mass at
death? at the end we are collections of objects to own and throw out
and pass/on. so what. the neighbours aren't allowed in the house. no
hugging. this antiseptic mourning must not be spoken aloud. so
what. his shaving kit. the cat piss. flowers in the garage. the goddamn
silver moon. i'm writing this from a windswept prairie town,
population 3,780. so what. so what. so what.

No Town Called Home

hey, it's your hometown calling
we've paved over the lyric "i"
cornered the market
on the word "expansion"

dear cat,

> *"what decade*
> *is it today,*
> *what century?"*

what poem
reinscribes wetlands
decimated by the Stoney Trail expansion?

we've got densification for days
rosy glasses
sandbags ready
prairie grasses waving in the shadows of
the function of the city and
the function of the cat

the Calgary streets
are paved with things
more harmful than oil:
thin blue lines
map Beltline's "no go" zones.

but all roads diverge
from Confluence Way
Jill Hartman's Simmons Building
and the Carpenters' Union Hall
of our youth

no metaphors for friendship
sizzle hot enough for billboards:

SAIT grads get jobs,
UNI grads go and

    ... heaven knows i'm bridgeable now ...

Toronto does not smell like Calgary
but the vacant cityscapes
in your Instagram feed
look identical to the scenes of my commute:

just nudge a tree over
remove the tram lines
the Subway and juice bar can stay.

is it too late
too gauche to admit
that i sold my mind to the company store

The Daily We

"The Daily We"

we need a new transitional object. click. we want new things to click
similar enough to the things we've already clicked to provoke a
feeling of security, but different enough to give our brain a fresh
dopamine buzz. the cat sneezes. click. can't tell if "resting
appropriate we" or "squandering time we." click.

"If We Become the Pariah"

even if there is no conviction
we didn't get a chance to Jane Lynch, son
O we rancid-absent ontology
no art but in erasure
we're making promises again without institutional backing
making promises inside Satan's wet-horse fever dream
lap alien innards
suck on the tailpipe of late capitalism's influencer culture

What you have, do we love it?
What we have, can you have it, too?
What you have, does it bring we peace?
What you have, can we sell it later?

"Let We Approach the Limit Case of This Nerve Ending"

this neighbourhood has changed without consent

let We approach the limit case of envy

let's bring everything back to 2007

it's hard to talk about social violence when we're all working
from downvoted definitions

i rode your mom's bike past the hospital where she died

i felt everything, we felt nothing, i'm a grease kid

let we equivocate:

i've just been informed that the barking dogs we heard this morning

were in fact doves

"Regress or Be Destroyed"

it is 1:11 a.m. and we are Tweeting about carbs. we have been baking
bread and sharing pictures of potatoes. someone is always talking
about yeast. who also rises? someone else already claims the
irrelevance of bread in 2020 because death-cult capitalism must
always name activities passé that hit mainstream uprising. the
capitalist engine needs us to fear our own obsolescence in the
identification of that which is over. "don't love the thing you
embraced yesterday." this is how we are kept trapped in an endless
consumptive cycle, eternally chasing The New. Marx told us, man.
he fucking warned us, bro. could the same be said for poetry. where
we once had a seat at the table of discourse, we no longer know the
terms of reference. this is what is known as the process of
elimination. our poetry elders have begun to die. was this what we
had planned for our one "wild and precious" life? i don't want this
anxiety of fading influence, don't want this culture that paves over
our many genealogies. i want to sit at the table of the elders, i want to
set a place for communal discourse. let me be the socially distant
potato you want to sit beside when next we are allowed to break
bread. it is 1:11 a.m. and we are mouthing tender creations for
tomorrow's feast.

We Have Finally Learned How to Contort When Rolling Over in Bed So as to Prevent the Cat from Leaving

A malevolent wind blows through Claresholm
a cursèd, migrainous prairie wind

"Anything properly applied can be a weapon
kindness can be a weapon"

We want to gather our dead into the house but
we'll need to bleach the place down first

One hundred more mouldy pants for the scientists

We thought you were on death's sour

Thank you for your hospitality slippers

There are no agents available for the first of the month

There's a knife with a trick i'm yearning to We

One day our fathers will be dead, so today we are eating
all the shortbread cookies they have baked

"Hello, devouring father"

We Still Want Eyelid Bees

"it's cloying, but we like it"

how many dead lawyers does me gotta
fellate to get
some renewable energy strategies around we?

cancel me, father, for we have sinned
this is our twelfth confession
and/or
i'm "sad" about "mass species death"
but we "still use plastic strips"
to "wax our back mole"
and/or
can we widen the focus a bit here?
and/or
we're "lonely" we
we're "late-cusp Gen X" me
we're "sincerely apathetic" we
bring we all your eyelid bees
let them feast on my globular warming tears

O petroleum
majestic apex of the patch
bring us all your eyelid bees
and set your We on fire

Heart Hunger Made Fashion

Touch down in the death space:
i celebrate myself, i glutton we.

Sleep is not the torture or the brain worms screaming

While Reykjavík burns, i organize we

A cat for every ailment
and two for grief and rage

i clothe myself, i embalm we

True horror lies in having any kind of body at all

i feed myself, i succour we
don't be sad about the cultural memory span; it's not for we

When in Claresholm the doves annoy
when i am gone we miss their keening

i feel myself, i solace we

May the hour of our death be appointed and painless
painless and appointment be the hour of our demise

i'm in the prairie, i burn we
let the soft animal of our body abandon love

Sidewalk copper afterimage of leaves
i mark myself, i catalogue we

Endless dispersal
wash your own mouth out with soap

i tax myself, i produce we

"New without tags" as refutation of mortality

i repeat myself, i unbutton we

"Fallen Metatarsals and the Infinite Sadness"

Lemon-gesso espresso depresso
i said where's the chiasmus in this, we said
where's the chiasmus in we

Shelter in Place

from the paper-still streets we see the reflection of flashing
emergency lights in the library windows. the father-in-law has picked
a fine time to start dying again. one hundred and twenty kilometres
away he counts morphine, plots a laundry chute escape, calls five
times a day with another thing he forgot. he forgot to say the
scientist stopped chemo when nail beds puffed toxic; one million
tiny crustaceans bloom. there's no planking these exponential
growth cats. we can't find an elegant metaphor for pain. inside we're
a bell-jar wasteland. we stay up late to google symptoms, check
temperatures. we ration toilet paper and rubbing alcohol. 35.5. does
the throat hurt. 36.2. what kind of cough was that. 35.4. we've
stopped counting panic attacks; the acid burn in the chest is from
stress bingeing. we say everything is terrible. we say this is fine.
falling into the twilight of the nap a malevolent voice bent close to
the ear, masculine and evil. breathed one word: *FAIL-WE.*

Pulmonary Mushroom Farming

our mother
came to say
the scientist found a spot
low in her lung
non-cancerous shape, dense
(CT scan inconclusive)
so they're doing a PET
when she leaves
i think
i would like to call my brother
instead i look out the window
at trees whose brothers i do not know
newly budding leaves
not yet green
stress eat bulk unsalted peanuts

try to be present to this moment
details on the leaves blurred out
the university health plan doesn't cover corrective lenses
so we need to wear these old off-focus contacts
to get my mushroom's worth

what kind of cat
doesn't know the name of common trees

it is 2019
the day after the provincial election
in little Texas
"the first incel premier"
someone said on Twitter

i harden my heart
enough
to withstand
the rise of far-right nationalism
i train my aging sick body
to fight?

this bulk unsalted peanut flings the fungal braying dove

Is It PTSD or Is It Cake?

O yes meticulous death cleaning

Yes we lifted endo belly

Yes we bloated gut balloon

Yes Climate is to Weather as Sex is to Death

Hello, Apocalypse?

It's we, Algernon

We muse on the professional liability that is grief

Yes we interrogate the position within the structure and

Yes we reinforce the structure and

Yes may we wrest this beam?

Mote meet eye

No Lazarus awakening

No vagus nerve vibrato

Yes scaley spiderweb nerves

Yes Pricklebody responds

This obituary is the best line

No this obituary is the best line

No words for past departures

What if Grandpa never got on that plane

Does it ache where the trauma lodges?

Changing his adopted sister's diaper

He witnessed her body freeze

Registered its meaning

Here's a legacy of the colonizer's hand:

Don't question what medicines we ingest

Don't question what medicines we stole

This is your inheritance, drink from

This path bifurcates a hundred times before we finish

Name the mushroom-thicket underbrush

Name a trail through the optic nerve

Name your choice of icing flavour

Name your chosen date of departure

Another Homage to the Mineral of Borscht

we bring potatoes, peel and slice thin.
no language here, no cabbage leaf on cheek.

back of her neck citrus and musk.

nun said *if she can't swallow the host,*
i have to wrap it in a tissue and burn it.

o flesh of my flesh. always scrubbing the pots.
you lose strength and cannot move.

none of us speak Ukrainian
no mother tongue to lick your face clean.

should have packed carrots and onions in a wheelbarrow.
filled your bed with vegetables and water.

she said remember when i used to pick you up from school
and take you out for lunch i'll never meet my great-grandchildren.

end of speech reduced to letter boards and blinking and periods.

i should have brought beets, sliced widthwise
pointed to the purple concentric rings.

did the scientist have to break your bones to straighten your hands?

we should have filled the casket with borscht, rye bread.
fresh laundry, Anaïs Anaïs, and cigarettes.

no language for amyotrophic lateral sclerosis.
the soul makes no sound when it leaves.

my brother said i think her brothers and sisters came
the room filled up with people.

After Crying at Urban Fare on December 31, 2019, in Calgary, Alberta

today's spring air smells coastal like Vancouver we. chinook or climate change? everyone is pregnant. we can't understand their optimism but i do their desperation. the air tastes fresh like hope and death, bergamot. no beginnings but in ending we. the album from Rena arrives in the post. on the cover her hand partly covers her face. my brother's ashes glitter the diamond on her right ring finger. the cat is bored and wants play but i'm back in bed already; one more nap to face the close of the decade we. no beginnings but in ending we. we know Urban Fare is bourgeois but it was on the way home. we were tired. i'm a class traitor on December 31, 2019, but in the wrong direction. in Claresholm the father-in-law is dying and in Calgary i've opened the window to let in the pseudo-sea air. we are facing the wrong way. Australia is on fire. none of we get out of this.

One Poet Always Lies

What Does It Mean to Occupy Land?

We moved to the country, learned stasis.

Birds bump their tiny heads on the windows.
Avoid milieus.

Cat sits transfixed. A place to pull apart
or rest. Chthonic signposts spell trouble.

In this house are three urns
two humans
two cats:
Seven souls in all.

Keep moving.

Leaves blow a crisp path around the door.

Avoid milieus.

Chthonic signposts spell trouble.
Seven souls in all.

Eldest millennials don't know
how to carve out a place called "home," only
dwellings so commodified that nobody lives there.

Shavings of heart can be found in every space we've paid to dwell.

Calgary will never
organize a rent strike.

People die and we occupy the rooms they've left behind.

We wanted continuity, got this shelf of dust.

For Christ's sake. Keep moving.

The brain makes its perambulations, and the owls are getting closer.

Women who are shaped like cows. Women who are cows:
"Bovine Implements of the Western Hemisphere."

Keep moving. Avoid milieus. The collective disbanded
too busy trying to shore up material security.

For Christ's sake, it's all leaked out of we.

Lost touch with the poets
forsook the comrades.

Forgive me, i'm sorry, forgive We

O brother you talk too much.

The elders are dead
we've thrown out their Tupperware.

Or the knock at the door was a woodpecker never
forget we're all going to die.

Keep on Truck

on 13th ave. near the last apartment
two old scientists load bricks
from a rusted ancient Silverado
into a wheelbarrow

passing through Upper Mount Royal
two cats practice
breakdancing
in a garage

on Richmond Road, painted on
a raised garden bed:
FLOURISH LOVE ♥ ATTENTION WE

turning the corner on 26th ave.
a blond wig in glitter

consciously enter the state of we
via this inherited truck
in the land of trucks and honey
to keep moving:
just keep moving

To the Maudlin Cats:

no chromosomes in foxholes or atheists at our kitchen sink. it's the
new Roaring Twenties. let's party like tech billionaires; ten days to
turn feral. turn tail on the timeline thirst traps and hunker down. we
thought you were really getting somewhere. here's the soft animal
death of the doomsday fatalists: no Russian submarines lurking in
the midst. no gorilla warfare in the streets. have an app, we've fired
the scientists. little petroleum's off his rocker and ranting sweet
bitumen. wet dream we; i'm drowning. fire the janitors and replace
them with autonomous drone scrubbers. but we're drowning. here's
a respirator joke. i'll make it funny; you know i can.

but we're drowning lungs, deck chairs through hourglass.
fire the cats and replace them with autonomous eyes.

But the Moon

Is the moon
But is the moon
What is the moon
What exactly did you think the moon was going to do for you, poet?
Why are you writing these words, line by line by line?
Towards what widening gyre do we turn, poet?
Do we abandon our friends, moving our slow thighs?
Letting the soft animal of our body abandon what it loves?
Crawling on our knees to the falconer daddy?
Letting the body animus of our softening
BUT IS THE MOON
Leading the animatronic heart of our body
Letting the soft dirty shirt of the distancing
Of the moon is the surface of the distance
Of the body POET WHERE HAVE YOU LEFT THE MOON
In the distance is the surface of the rough beast
WHAT HAVE YOU DONE WITH MY SOFT ANIMAL BODY

Fear Is, Um, Part of Love

an insect's eye is how we begin
we're thick with it
fear with

riotous cones and rods
how we melt into it
sick with

worry into muddled
now you see
not fear but

one dozen refractions of
the other's body

blink again, whoops
followed one dozen arms
to their logical conclusion
now we don't

Rain. Cloud. Rain.

the cats go back to bed

the cats are not friends

the cats, who are not friends, must be kept in separate rooms
lest they rip and tear
with tooth and claw
each other's soft bellies

outside the magpies screech

the cat must call a tree company

i do not mean to imply
cozy domesticity

inside we are all cozily caged
the cat buys vegetables and cooks them

today there is a summer storm warning

groceries cost four times what they did ten years ago

the cat is thinking of making a stir-fry

no decisions are neutral

rain. cloud. rain.

Communing with the Cats

ugh that was awful, we say,
i was horrible!

the trains will be stopping to separate

we could create some real art here if only we could quiet thoughts

soften up edgy in old age

the orchestra will not produce good music

my neck, we say, my carpal tunnel syndrome

painbody vibrato of sciatic and tibial

everyone collectively decided careerism was cool again
but nobody sent me the memo?

it's good
it's not good
it doesn't push past the gimmick

    – *mind the gap* –

four hundred pages is too long i don't have that kind of attention span

we like this or that new work
we like that new cat
we don't like the books that we tell each other to like

is it good? should i read it?
what are you working on?
should i read it?

We Miss "Community"

woke from a dream about the promise we squandered to be
something real back in 2003, and an excavation of storage in which
we found a stuffed bear that smelled like Baba. we're sorry for my
sour feelings. there's no poetry inside the brains of fake Mennonites.
there's no poetry inside the brains of migraineurs. there's too much
poetry inside the brains of neurodivergents. there's no poetry inside
the brains of digital communicators. there's no poetry inside the
brains of leftist Albertans. there's too much poetry inside the brains
of the grieving. there's no poetry inside the brain under green light.
there's no poetry inside the brains of the settler state. there's too
much poetry. there's no poetry inside the brains of the chronically ill.
we have tried and failed one million times to think myself back to
health. it is false that no one loves me and it is true that no one loves
we. there is no community inside the dream. the cats run to the next
energetic field; survivors comb the abandoned landscape for scraps.

Morning Meditation

Gently hold whatever arises
and when you're ready
let it go:

Ghost telephones from distant shores,
the rise of bile in the throat
rattlesnake venom coursing through the dog.

Observing the fluctuations of the mind, i saw:
vertical sperm whales stacked seven layers deep.
The ribbon worm's proboscis
rhizoming half the length of a human arm
white tree root toxins stake their claim.

Clouds drift as they must
rattlesnake venom courses through the dog.
You crawl through the desert on your knees,

Gently hold whatever arises

THE MESSENGER

i am/two white horses/a part
in a line/could be worse/we awaken radically on fire/
transformed onboard
in the charnel ground/sister bone
a part of life/take off my hooves
stoic messenger/and a part
if i took your place/of you
and burn/would it hurt/them

skin/potato/ash/and a part
leave your bags/affix your own oxygen
embrace change/mask/in all forms
a part/abandon personal belongings
a part of life/step off the platform
a part of life/radically burned clean
a part engorged inferno
and a part of you

Plants We Have Killed

what duty of care do we owe each other?

when embodiment stands in
for direct action?

if gentle theft is when we hold your lines
in my mouth

measure the resiliency of the basil
branching towards the east window
each leaf's bosom lifts to the sun

what is the self
outside of relationality

basic unit of composition: irritation

vestibular tipping
brain thinks we're falling again

we've murdered another succulent

and when did the future lose its sense of expanse
sitting here at midlife
swollen fingers, proto-jowls, skin creases at every joint

twenty years spent trying and failing
to write a poem to match the jouissance

of my favourite indie pop songs

somewhere, friends
inhabit other cities
commute to their jobs
we don't meet for coffee

no object holds a solid edge
table: wavy
plant pot: wavy

"ah daddy i wanna be drunk many days"

we wanna be this anonymous animal for the rest of my life

the young barista skips around the Braids record:

> the one about solitude
> the one about lust
> the one about rape culture

it's a Wednesday, early August
yesterday's scratchy throat a portent
of today's smoky skies
fell into the decade without enough protest
no flânerie at midlife
just bills! bills!
physiotherapy
anxiolytics for our neuropathy

earlier watched a fly on my Lisa Robertson
carefully clean front legs, then back
wipe down each wing
always want to use the word "thorax"
for ribcage
we, too, long to lift off with vestigial wings

there's no post-pandemic
commons
just panic and yelling
pack your things and go
every other week

what duty of care do we owe each other
towards healing the mother-wound
when we can't even keep our houseplants alive

Dialectical Behavioural Poetry 1:

situations that elicit painful emotions

whose mortality is more painful to confront:

whose security makes you vulnerable:

whose comfort is more painful:

> we choose to confront our generation
> we choose not to confront our generation

instead of friends, a series of blinking avatars
we send love letters disguised as memes

it's 2020 and the cells of our body are heavy with the city's cancer

we turn forty
take up weed smoking
holy smoke, relics of past sins
no time like the present to make
an altar inside our body

Dialectical Behavioural Poetry 2:

situations that are avoidable,
but avoidance can cause other problems in our lives

Dear Poetry,

Whose saga is not political?

Is it morally defensible to purchase that plane ticket?
How will we do penance for our carbon footprint? What burden we?
Reading or breeding we? The supermarket me?

What comes first: painbody me? shamebody we?

Might we be mid-trilogy cats?

Dialectical Behavioural Poetry 3:

chronic problem situation – ongoing issue
that creates a state of misery
is continual
and most often in need of solving

the whole body grows in whorls
toenails embed skin
hair spiral dermis
pubic mound endometria
deviation from spherical curvature
which results in distorted images
as light rays are prevented from meeting
at a common focus

a bloated apex deviation:
spiral roughly human-shaped

at what age did we realize
painful bowel movements weren't our
common focus
there's no poetry in the painbody
no poetry in the painbody
where's the dignity in the four-times-disabled shamebody
diagnosis radiculitis we said yes, it is ridiculous

the iLL symbolic

Monday

A blown
beautiful prosody
romantic menacing
morning

The flickers view undertones
we fence

A little bluish constitution

Checkered shadow
it consumes
more stigmata
cold wintry dribble

Think "historical"

Day's estrangements
about interest

We sex synthetics
that frequently
open

So stated
some long the many
purse-soaking night
authors migraines

A
rain

A
day

We soul-thrilling antiquity

Peculiar lift
power-lapsing

Hovers some description
we present specific

A drink-day migraine

Us ripple It personality

Light ruffles back
concerned

The lustily
cigarette usually
so portrayed

Flattering as
mist star

Exchange obsessive
contact

Picture rigid
our driving
surface

A surplus
the perfectionistic
the sharp

A migraineur and
land frost
very *Perhaps*

So pull and great one forth out
a tide may

The night-lurid
dull fall conditions this
mist of enter tendency this
comes snow as concept this
rolling our may
mind from this

This measured west
most by
this skin

Certain writers

A delicacy on

Clinical slight
or migraine finding
imaginary cloud

Grace suffer
adulthood drifts there
exceedingly contrary

Migraine-varied glaze to signs
emotional

Which all backgrounds
lift planet
indicate events in

This day

We're of accounts constitution iLL
paper snow exemplifies

Monday

The open May phalanx
lighter perception Its arousal

We noted
the clouds
the scotoma nervous
darker paresthesia melting

Expand ever brevity
heart flickering
the plain darker nausea
catharsis fully painstaking

But history or malaise
darker never blue

A drowsiness

Worshipped parity
the grief-Rage
and emotional fluid

It crumbles
darker the engorgement
muscular symptoms

Sometimes slackness
conveniently vascular

Bottom-stuccoed
top clouds

The weakness stage

Days over like lighter prodrome

And heap Half-dense
sometimes similar rebound
typical cloudfog bottom
simply troubles us

Half Days plain
where plain is heap

Half migraine-related cloud

Half human

The resolution compact in love

Plain Memory-Pushing sequence
feeling largely flows Utopia

True crumbles plain
crumbles visceral
abruptly euphoria
parts us open

Renewed
selected emotional scorn
one terms "stasis"
anticipated clouds
plagiarize excitement and shame

Looking cloudy

Like excitation on alert

Attack with ejaculation

Arousal which, causality
bottom-crumbles herself

Except open the symptoms

All sky clouds
synchronization
between symptoms

Days darker
causing emotional sneezing
affect somatic
built upon
the provocative or emotional
others on us

Plain stimulus
somatic emotional symptoms
smaller Where
part sudden symptoms

Except loveliness is internally excess
allows vice

We Grace darker by prostration

Fallen in the aura isolated
into sadness by deferring
others

Gradually Love crumbles
bottom emotional

And the Days subsidized open

Where clouds transgression

Given later is possible
plain rage, which
variety, time
part elation

The ill Symbolic

In bottom publicly and/or
affective secretory terms

When linkage
mobilizes other activities

No dream is diuresis

The sky horror

The us It bottom

Monday

Towards scotoma we come
with apertures preferring Nothing

Throw wallpaper and ludicrously else
closes inadequate glittering

We honeycomb We're suddenly slapping
observe images clinical

When now gulls
be dazzling and walk shimmering

Now also blown jets
close formulation surface

Here eyes equally water
absurd-bend offered still

Come we agitated
visible theories We

A more crawling
few faintly

Now when minutes crisp
later come

And this eyes histories

We fall accompanied open

Now When It sparkle-worthy
a last chapter eating walking

Vibration twenty indicate
Now When It swagger-hung

The thirty-richness drinking falling
right minutes and

Now When hand transmit
as were aura smelling calm

If Now eating It
by It yellow

When sucking resting splitting

When Spring on headache rare

We the Structure to mass want
sounding encounter

Come to board we speak
of Aura single

When belts piano
by the light dots

When flashes and come It
moving misunderstood

We come slowly because migraine
now across the aura

Ignoring regulating When drinking
field thought in clouds

When monogamous vision
is common

Come besieged Patterns
now tripping

When conditions suddenly reveal

When changing that freedom none

Images common come

When flowers or cormorants pip
a play of raying equated dozen

When wet with manifestations
corn stillness opening

All comes out
headache around

When Everything is dogs' aspect
faceted a lick

Account and migraine mould

When auras multiplied
aura of newness
bubbles with distance

And rising Come shame

/my symptom/

    /our symptom/
    /you symptom/
    /It symptom/

My ill symbolic
our iLL symbolIC
your III symBOLic

Symptomatic you're illin'

We ill cymbal-ic
you i'll cymbalta
the ILL tsymbaly

Ill spill thrill shambolic pill
inside this feast

The iLL imbolC

Monday

First bright breach appearing semantic
with belief and greeny-blue
strong surrounding entry into paradise

The syllable by the field into

The definition of pliable

Pours all bursting allied strange
out across the phenomena and
medium space

The bright term, the sick
a swathe-formed belief
migraine-only world

Time light clear boundaries
not red fleece and stretched

Unmistakable roominess-laid rant

Witty to exist but long bright out

And the unanalyzable roar
famous breaking feeling

Transparency fresh fraying
fine point which caused
bright rope and impulse

Something grand the
conveyance of copper
fresh stormy centre forced wrong

Bright beech and belief
so to this rupture
behind bright violent
adopt a fresh-crested
subtle sparkling aluminum

And open we nosological by transport
and catalpa turbid clarity

Scant wet silver

Raging place

And clamour common clinical
rare and bright privation

Migraine action when deep
tint It very clear

We in We entire fine construct speaks

The range spring-spoken belief
indisputable such opulent
intransigent boundaries

Each morning spacious after this attack

Blissful fields came
hard battlement tops us

Hot group
and trick of belief
the general slender

Celebrate lustful migraine
feeling scarce fast
equivalents of bright tint

Eager polymorphous disorder
quotidian silver
the curious Itself teaches

Ribbons sky before manifestations
the temperate and sure beauty

Should migraine begin failing

Light be
patient afresh

To wind dear bright various
decompositions though general realms fine

Dear afresh and discordant afresh
so agglomerates purposes morbid

The grand undersides
so calmly of feeling atmosphere

The free and different exposition
that sky leaves to clear migraine
and encompasses heaven

Earth-flawed brushed leaf

We present intimation and part praise
sure, must migraine terraqueous

We're behind We recognize
dear a migraine, there tumbling

We penumbra so fully appearing

First believe
sing floating the very last elevated
near heavenly fine with analogous
rustling belief

Lust reactions
symptoms peculiar, flimsy apricot

Just thin clear landscape
bright frill stiff We speak

As pure scarce hot bias ambition
and migraine enters

Flesh swoop we clear
appearing deeper and near
hue the last duty

Our sullen spacious title
and dread skies
bloated trees

A fresh syndrome landscape
part beautiful

Quotas silver and elegant and defined
not more forgeries
the dear and artificial
fine brisk edges

Fine but streaky footing

We diffuse to Nothing

Enter outward The face
grand massed brisk

Until suffering

Fresh meaningful changing belief
patient migraine and lively merges

Monday

Maybe meadows squandering deep
here on visceral
truncated activities

Find a woods
here loam almost flesh
line upon crosses and
physical It vomit
late strong chalk

Here quit will terminated
reverse line

Here when activity may

Here the workfall causes
adrenaline home

Here the exercise mates on emotion farms

We hill last then prevent attacks
terminate shout
and luck close

Here Here Here It may
exist

Attack minutes
equally
early
manors

Here were seconds up
or
arm wrestling
and day has a headache

Both Sunday mines
new house set its occurrence
its enclosures upon
here accomplish

Many Sudden
fright effective
rising woods

The gratification of chalk edge

Here to avert
classical
and disperse

Forests here
system or migraines get time

Three patients or houses
sand pours

Yet so patient
violent
and here
basin
from visible
deliciously
various forms

An effective example
wake in
hard streets

Its remains ulterior
patients have attack

Here two canal-mouth
here work rage-displace

Here We first will
ask temperament
a physical hill

Tongues attack church design

Maybe attack within comes here

Here migraine dell
is a gaze interchange
or end

Lie or fight

Here nameless a flickering

Here how employs

Here church

Here waiting cause

Paroxysmal
or five other
a
migraine
hill

Here is here
and mine is dell

Its effect

Violent drinking
with

Violent
abed

A desolation-crossed Work

It coitus
run around

Monday

Hard pink road
our thousands end
takes illness work

Such language riddling
mistake contemplation
half-intervals

The end requires
patient rain years
there unexpected

We the Disease

Our landscape's face accomplished road

Long objects
which disburdening
the group's pulling cloth
who, wanting such rain
diagnosis alone
unlearn migraine affliction

What understands Migraine necessity
only miserable passing

Not Just

Epilogue striving detours

Next To nothing for
migraine the clangour

Physicianly heart
but golden end of
patient
ignorant

A height is Migraine
less windy

Long patient's
perplexed
mild multiplying terrifying
phoneme

And

The Land's fearful knowledge

Own miseries you
vernaculars blazing one's
name falsity absolution
gleams causation hard

When

Short infinite
device
now quicken We
dark life

We come stressed fine
the imperative love book
stubborn strange
Town Me Fear You
the all follows is
usually surface

Lung Short we fear the Road
scarcely know our patient

Monday

The amazing repeated recall
by upward structures

Storms in patient fibres plumped

Cited collapsing Construct winds
hot or uninhabitable
humid twenty-five

On streets classical whose erotic examples

Here classical-heart-love and the
provocative attacks resist

Body should come
cloud number after
persons arrive

Be construed violently
breaking their competitive
maximum claim cross-country

Not the meteorological listlessness no
enough bafflement clairvoyance

Great and prostrated time

Pleasure empty states

We ballrooms must
they favour make

Thrice future predict
appear in We the Dust

This advance water context
and which zestful
maybe alabaster applied pigment

Hallucinations willy-nilly
or confession stainless distort many

Steel impending conflict

Construct thunder unneedful
from spurious odder
and most radical banality

Its "idiosyncratic" suffer circumstances
the hurts possess sometimes
distant-felt men

Held world

New times
forbidding golden

Within ourselves

Body
attacks

Rival cloud tells
excitement that

Body personified me

Emotion is

Violent cloud

We abandon that
a childhood marred

Its organic argument
at nature sensitivity
sexual is certain

May peninsula lost times
elements Body

We mimicked Rest

Both by cloud
on which occurred

Living the fringe
would bottom the excitement

Annual buildings
vigorous southwesterly
often pathological

How architecture gales
habit
is FRIDAY

Inclement, which
namely

It
Weather
Blow
Now

Any unique conditioned
reflex
be all and
a climatic
lady

Tacit
never younger

Like the rose
attack fever

We attack time

Rarely a
sorrow or paper
rose

We
speak

My dad asked if the last poem would make its way into my next book. i said no man can know the future.

In the quiet we hear the ocean in my own ear, a gentle rush. When we panic, it roars. Can we slow the rate of change down to the pace of cellular regeneration. Can we embrace a fade to graceful obscurity. Can we ensure our communities have everything they need? In Claresholm my spouse tacks up a tarp to block the sun so they can look in at their father in his hospital bed. Their ice-fishing suit keeps out the early prairie spring. When we conference call, he proudly tells his nurse that he's having a three-way. No one has the heart to let him know we're huddled here in the space where it stings. We are waiting to be raptured. *No man can know the future.*

Notes on the Text

This book is for, after, and with Ryan Fitzpatrick, Danielle LaFrance, Simon Brown, Roger Farr, Lisa Robertson, Fred Wah, Cobra Collins, Taylor Lambert, and countless other poet and writer comrades, collaborators, and disruptors.

No Town Called We was written between 2018 and 2022, during which time "I" grappled with the somatic experience of chronically ill embodiment in the chronically ill city. These poems grasp after the communal "we."

This book is situated on stolen Indigenous Land in places "we" now call Calgary (Mohkínstsis / Wîchîspa Oyade / otôskwanihk ᐅᒎᖸᣆᓂᔅ / Guts'ists'i / ʔaknuqtap¢ik / Klincho-tinay-indihay) Claresholm (located on the Traditional Territories of the Siksikaitsitapi ᖹᒍᐧᄀ [Blackfoot Confederacy], Îyârhe Nakoda, and Tsúùt'ínà), Montréal (Tiohtià:ke / Mooniyaang), Baltimore (located on the Traditional Territories of the Susquehannock and Piscataway Conoy), and in the space the critic Tiziana Terranova refers to as the "Corporate Platform Complex."

Danielle LaFrance performed a necessary intervention towards the poet's intentions, his coming community, her hive-mind milieu, their pathologies.

The cats in these poems act as companion animals, as poets, as critics, as friends and keepers of city knowledge and shared history. Ryan Fitpatrick is "the cat" named in "We Wonder If i Will Ever Manage to Write a Poem about Heat Death" and "No Town Called Home."

"We Wonder If i Will Ever Manage to Write a Poem about Heat Death" and "We ♥ Alberta's Ol' Symbolic" refer to the climate-change fires in Australia in 2019. The City of Calgary declared a climate emergency in 2021. By 2022, the city had thirty-nine new communities in progress, with another eight at the outskirts up for approval. The city's sprawl continues a pattern of unsustainable growth.

In "Oil and Gas Don't Love We Back," the reference to waydowntown continues an homage to the Gary Burns film of the same name, as seen in my chapbook *Behind the Drywall*. "All hell for a basement" was Rudyard Kipling's reported comment upon a visit to Medicine Hat. Alberta's Ralph Klein government blew up the old Calgary General Hospital in 1998 as a cost-saving measure. By 2022, the province was, like many Canadian provinces, experiencing a health-care crisis.

In "No Town Called Poetry," "the era of the spectacle" and "the coming community" are from Giorgio Agamben's *The Coming Community*.

"We are bipedal fuckups whose cells start to eat themselves if we live too long" is an aphorism spoken by my friend Igpy Kin. Used with permission.

Fred Wah encouraged his 2000–2001 cohort of poetry-writing students at the University of Calgary to interrogate what was at stake in our poems with the question "So what?" I interrogate my poem's speaker with it here, with thanks and apologies.

In "No Town Called Home," the lines *what decade / is it today, / what century?* are from ryan fitzpatrick's *Coast Mountain Foot*. Jill Hartman's *A Painted Elephant* is referenced. The Carpenter's Union Hall has been torn down and is now condos.

Danielle LaFrance provided the last line for "Regress or Be Destroyed." The line "Marx told us, man. he fucking warned us, bro" in this poem is modified from the meme "*I fucking warned you dude. I told you bro A CRITICAL ANALYSIS OF CAPITALIST PRODUCTION BY KARL MARX.*"

In "We Have Finally Learned How to Contort When Rolling Over in Bed So as to Prevent the Cat from Leaving," the line "Anything properly applied can be a weapon / kindness can be a weapon" is spoken by the character Ashford in *The Expanse*, season 4, episode 10, "Cibola Burn." "Hello, devouring father" is from MC Hyland's *The End*.

"Another Homage to the Mineral of Borscht" is an elegy for my baba and steals from Erín Moure's poetic framing of Ukrainian lineage and root vegetables.

"What Does It Mean to Occupy Land" was partly inspired by Roger Farr's book *After Villon*, and owes to his lines, "Keep moving. Avoid milieus // & for Christ's sake never / forget we're all going to die."

"But the Moon" is after all the poets you think it is.

"Fear Is, Um, Part of Love" is for and after Simon Brown, from his above/ground chapbook *oh the iffy night*.

"THE MESSENGER" was commissioned for katie o'brien's *Blood Orange* poetry tarot project and steals from Beck, Chad VanGaalen, the Dodos, Child Actress, Pema Chödrön, and a button I bought from Shelf Life Books containing the text: "I am death / a part of life / and a part of you."

In "Plants We Have Killed," the line "ah daddy i wanna be drunk many days" quotes Frank O'Hara misquoting John Weiners.

Mary Oliver is bastardized in several poems, with thanks and apologies.

"The iLL Symbolic" takes lines from Lisa Robertson's *The Weather* and Oliver Sacks's *Migraine*, and weaves, refracts, dilates, shatters, honeycombs them into a poetics of migraine, a disease I have suffered from for thirty-one of my forty-three years, and a disease which primarily affects those assigned female at birth. These lines are also written with love for Élèn Kainz, Lucia Lorenzi, and Heather Buchanan.

Acknowledgments

Versions of the following poems have appeared in the following
places:

"We Wonder If i Will Ever Manage to Write a Poem about Heat
Death" and "We ♥ Alberta's Ol' Symbolic" on Watch Your Head.

"This Is Not My Beautiful Horse," "So What," and "After Crying at
Urban Fare on December 31, 2019, in Calgary, Alberta" in the /tƐmz/
Review.

"Pulmonary Mushroom Farming," the three "Dialectical Behavioural
Poetry" poems, "Goodnight Capital," "We Have Finally Learned
How to Contort When Rolling Over in Bed So as to Prevent the Cat
from Leaving," and "But the Moon" in the chapbook Softbody
(Toronto/Tkaronto: Model Press, 2021).

"Who Do We Serve," "So What," and "To the Maudlin Cats:" on Ice
Floe Press.

"If we become the pariah" in Chaudiere Books' blog.

"I Still Want Eyelid Bees" in Watch Your Head: Writers & Artists
Respond to the Climate Crisis (Toronto: Coach House Books, 2020).

"Let We Approach the Limit Case of This Nerve Ending." in n-o-b-o-d-y 1
(spring 2020).

"THE MESSENGER" in Blood Orange poetry tarot project.

Thanks to the editors for supporting my work.

Gratitude to Catriona Strang, Kevin Williams, Leslie Smith,
Charles Simard, Erin Kirsh, Darren Atwater, Spencer Williams,
Vicki Williams, and Rya at Talonbooks.

Photo by Heather Saitz

NIKKI REIMER (she/her/they/them) is a multimedia artist and writer and chronically ill neurodivergent prairie settler currently living in Mohkínstsis/Calgary. She has been involved with arts and writing communities, primarily in Calgary and Vancouver, for over twenty years. They are the author of four books of poetry and multiple essays on grief. GRIEFWAVE.com, a multimedia, web-based, extended elegy, was launched in February 2022. Frequent themes Reimer explores through their work include feminism, the body, the Anthropocene, late capitalism, death, grief, loss, and animal subjectivity.

Though their practice began in the literary arts, Reimer's artistic work has taken turns into multiple forms of interdisciplinary artmaking, including visual art and video, installation work, and performance practice. Reimer's work has been extensively reviewed, often noting their embrace of dark humour and feminist refusal.

Visit reimerwrites.com / cjjrlegacyfund.com / @NikkiReimer.